WALKS IN THE

Derwent
Valley

by Tim Deveaux

First published in Great Britain as a softback original in 2015

Second Edition 2018

Typeset in Minion Pro

Editing, design and publishing by UK Book Publishing

UK Book Publishing is a trading name of Consilience Media

www.ukbookpublishing.com

ISBN: 978-1-910223-41-3

Contents

Introduction

This is the second edition of a book describing 11 walks in the beautiful
Derwent valley in County Durham. All walks have been rewalked and some
minor changes made to the walk description to reflect changes in the
environment and to make the descriptions a little clearer. The routes vary from
3.7 to 10 miles, but are mostly of moderate difficulty based on a fairly fit 64 year
old!! There are some walks which need to be done on a good weather day e.g.
walk 11.

Part of the Derwent valley is in an area of outstanding natural beauty and
there are some stunning views of the whole valley and some unexpected
features throughout the walks.

The walks include a number of descriptions of the places visited in each
walk. I hope this helps to enhance the walks even more than the beautiful places
they show you.

I have also included a wide range of refreshment hostelries where you may
want to take a well earned break! Many are coffee and tea stops but there are
some with stronger tipples. I tend to go for either a coffee and bacon sandwich
or a pint of real ale!

Wildlife and landscape

These walks give you an opportunity to appreciate the variety of landscapes in
the valley. There are woodland walks, woodland and open field walks, walks
with waterfalls, walks in wild moorland, walks with some fantastic wood
carvings, and all the walks go near the river!!

The valley is also home to a large number of Red Kites. These impressive
birds can be seen every day in the skies above Rowlands Gill and the Derwent
Walk. You may hear their screech call before you see them but once you do you
will be greatly impressed by their size and beauty.

There are a wide range of habitats in the valley – woodlands, meadows,
wetlands, riverside and reclaimed industrial sites.

In the woodlands you will see wood anemones and celandines in spring.
Butterflies such as the common blue and meadow brown can be seen in the
meadows. There are many birds including green woodpecker, great spotted
woodpecker, nuthatch and bullfinch, mistle thrush and song thrush. There are

several hunting birds including sparrowhawk. You may also see fox, badger and roe deer. On and in the River Derwent itself you may see kingfisher, dipper and otter.

Maps and rights of way

Most walks follow public footpaths and bridleways with some following roads, some quiet and some with a modest amount of traffic. These pathways are signposted, mostly, when leaving a road. There are some permissive paths. Sometimes moor tracks are used but these are usually public rights of way. I have tried to use public rights of way off road where possible but where there is no alternative roads are used. Please use the paths and grass verges where indicated.

Each walk is circular and is provided with an approximate distance, an assessment of difficulty, estimated time and starting point which is always the end point. A map of each walk is also provided to guide you through the walk in addition to the description of the route. It is advisable that you take an Ordnance Survey map with you to double check your route in case you go wrong. I hope this is unlikely!!!! I used the OS Explorer series maps for the routes.

Clothing and footwear

Wear sturdy shoes but preferably walking shoes or boots. It can be muddy at certain times of the year so be prepared. Gaiters will be useful for some walks and warm comfortable socks will make the experience much more pleasurable. Always take a waterproof top and if you feel it necessary waterproof trousers. The British weather is notoriously fickle!

Some of the moors walks can be cool or even downright cold. So look at the weather forecast and make a judgement about what you feel comfortable in wearing.

Safety

Some walks are near the river so be very careful when you get close to the riverbank. Non-slip shoes or boots are useful for most walks. Walks over the moors can be risky if the weather is poor or changeable. Do them on a good weather day. If you are an experienced walker your clothing will cope with most scenarios.

Respect for the countryside

Leave the countryside how you find it. Close gates where they are closed, leave them open if they are open. Take litter home. Keep to the route. You will come across cattle, sheep and horse. Always treat them with respect and caution. Some can be a little feisty!

If you have a dog with you, always keep it under control and on a lead when near livestock.

Some walks go through Areas of Outstanding Natural Beauty and some through sites of special scientific interest. Please leave them as you find them!

Walk 1: Derwenthaugh Park

Distance	4.6 miles
Time	2 hours
Difficulty	Moderate mainly due to steps.
Parking	Winlaton Mill car park off the A694 opposite the garage.

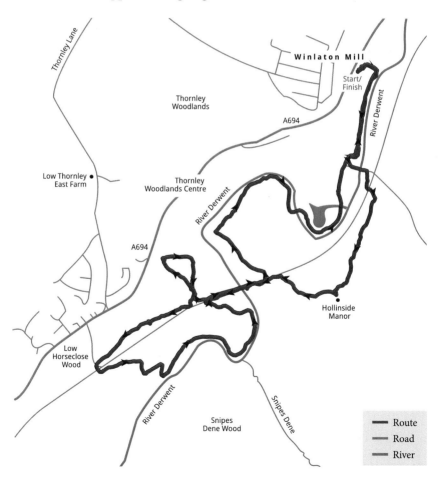

Start

Facing away from the road and garage go to the left corner of the car park to enter the Red Kite walk (not that we are doing the Red Kite walk – just part of it!). This takes you behind the visitor centre.

Follow this to the path near the river and turn right to follow the tarmac track past a dog walking area and the rear entrance to the Red Kite pub.

Butterfly Bridge

Continue for about 200 to 300 metres until the track goes right then left (dog leg). Turn left toward the Butterfly bridge over the River Derwent. Cross over the bridge.

Hollinside Manor

Over the bridge turn right to the multi user route. Follow the directions to the Derwent Walk. Go up the steps onto the Derwent Walk. Cross over the walk immediately in front of you to the path to Hollinside Manor. Carry on up some steep steps, follow the trail through woodland until it bears right past a fence in a corner of field, and follow the fenceline with a farm in the distance.

On the right is a woodland of oak, holly, birch, sycamore, beech and hawthorn.

Go past a gate to the farm; within 100 metres you'll find Hollinside Manor. Take the left path past the manor, continuing to the path going downhill on some very steep steps. At the bottom of the steps is a wooden walkway across a boggy field.

You eventually come to a stile. Cross over it and head down the hill, down some steps through woodland. In about 50 metres you come to a gate, go through the gate onto the Derwent walk and turn left towards the viaduct, 100 metres away. Cross the viaduct.

Gibside

Pause on the viaduct to glory at the wonderful views of the Statue of British Liberty, the River Derwent, Gibside and the meadows adorning the river.

Sculpture park

About 100 metres past the end of the viaduct turn right about 30 metres before the picnic tables through the gate. In about 20 metres there are a set of steps to your right. Climb the steps to the top and bear left along the track.

In about 30 metres there is a wooden sculpture of a frog and a snake to your right. Continue on the path to a second wood sculpture, a badger; in a further 40 metres is a toadstool sculpture. At the junction in the path, turn right past the otter sculpture on the left. Further on is a butterfly and stag beetles are on your right. Follow the path down to the right past a low fence on the left and within 20 metres is a sculpture of an owl and a further 30 metres a sculpture of a red kite in the clearing on the right.

In a further 30 metres you return to the top of the steps you came up, go down the steps, at the bottom bear right, then, in about 10 metres, turn left to the gate. When through the gate turn right along the Derwent walk, but immediately on your right go up the track signposted 'Viewpoint'.

Gibside again

The path goes uphill and on your left you can see the Derwent Walk. At the top of the hill you come to some steps that dip down and then up, and within about 30 metres views of Gibside start to open up. You first see the Statue of British Liberty and then Gibside Hall.

Carry on the path which goes downhill eventually to a gate. Go through the gate and turn left over a bridge over the Derwent walk and then at the T junction turn left along the tarmacked road. Carry on to the newly refurbished farm buildings on the left and a gate on your right. Go through the gate and bear right down the track. This area is usually home to a few horses – take a little care, they are usually placid so don't worry about them. Dog owners, please put them on leads.

The meadows

This track winds downhill for a couple of hundred metres till you come to a gate. Go through the gate and onto a grassy path. Turn right to a path along the river side. Follow this for about 150 metres and it brings you out to a large meadow. Turn right along the path that follows the line of the river to some steps. Go up the steps and bear right to continue to follow the line of the river for a few hundred metres.

Eventually you follow the path to bear left away from the river to a grassy area through a gap in the hedge. With the red walking man sign on the left bear right. The path narrows to go through shrubbery and left up the hill with the viaduct on your right. Follow the waymarking posts and well worn path and turn right up to a gate and some steps. Go up the steps where you find the Derwent walk again. Turn right and cross the viaduct.

'Teletubby land' and the lake

About 50 metres past the end of the viaduct there is a sign 'Newcastle C2C', turn left to follow the tarmacked path. There are three tracks here. The right one goes down to a bridge over the river and is a short cut compared to the track to the left. The central track goes through the woodland / meadow area known locally as 'Teletubby land' or 'Goodshields' as it is signposted. If you take this one it will bring you out to the tarmacked path on the left further down.

Take the left track keeping the River Derwent on your left. In about 500 metres you will come to a bridge, cross it and turn right and go around the lake with the river now on your right hand side.

Home

Continue on the tarmacked path and pass the Butterfly bridge on your right. Continue along the walk and retrace your steps past the dog walk and the Red Kite pub on your left back to the car park, or alternatively you could enjoy a well earned drink at the pub!

Information

Refreshments

At the *Red Kite* pub, open from 12.00 to 11.00pm everyday with food served all day from 12.00 to 8.30pm. *The Red Kite*, Spa Well Road, Winlaton Mill, Blaydon on Tyne NE21 6RU Tel. 0191 414 5840

Cafe at Thornley Woods is open to the public from: 10am-2pm Monday to Friday, 1pm-4pm Saturday and Sunday. Tel. 01207 545212

Land of Oak and Iron Visitors Centre, Spa Well Road, Winlaton Mill Located on the A694 near Rowlands Gill. Toilets, parking, visitor help, displays and information are available.

Hollinside Manor

Hollinside Manor is a 13th century manor house. It was the home of the Harding family for two centuries during which time the manor became known as the 'Giant's Castle', since the men folk were very tall. The estate passed on to George Bowes of Gibside in 1730 for the sum of £10,000. Today the Manor is an Ancient Monument.

Derwenthaugh Park

Until 1986, Derwenthaugh Park was the site of the Derwenthaugh Coke Works. Opened in 1928 it took coal from the Chopwell colliery and the resulting coke was shipped from the staithes on the River Tyne at Derwenthaugh. In the 18th and 19th centuries Crowley's Ironworks dominated the site. These were the largest ironworks in Europe at the time. The workers lived in old Winlaton Mill which was situated along the lane beside the Red Kite pub. The village was demolished and re-built on its present site in 1937.

Derwent Valley Railway

The Derwent Valley Railway was opened in 1867 after three years' hard building work. Four viaducts were constructed and a deep, 800 metres long cutting was dug near Rowlands Gill. Stations were built at Shotley Bridge, Ebchester, High Westwood, Lintz Green, Rowlands Gill and Swalwell. At its peak the railway was carrying over half a million passengers a year with regular goods traffic of timber, bricks and coal to Newcastle and iron ore to Consett.

As road traffic became more efficient the service declined until the line finally closed in 1962. The railway is commemorated in the Geordie folk song about an ill-fated train journey from Rowlands Gill, 'Wor Nanny's a Mazer'.

Nine Arches Viaduct

The Nine Arches Viaduct was one of the major engineering feats of the railway. It is five hundred feet long and was built because the Earl of Strathmore would not allow the railway to pass through the Gibside Estate.

The Butterfly Bridge and Winlaton Mill

The Butterfly Bridge was originally built in 1842 by John English. Lang Jack, as he was known, stood 6 feet 4 inches and worked as a stonemason on the old Scotswood Bridge before he built the Butterfly Bridge. The new bridge was built in 1950 but it was swept away in the floods of 2008. The current bridge was put in place in 2011. Near the bridge are the remains of George Eavan's house, the miller of the flour mill. This ruin is all that remains of old Winlaton Mill. The village was very attractive with white-washed cottages and a stream running through the centre. Winlaton Mill was founded by Saxon families who chose to settle there after the Romans left the area.

It is thought that Cromwell's army of 16,000 men crossed the Derwent River here on the 15th July 1650 on their way to the Battle of Dunbar.

'Teletubby land'

When the Derwenthaugh Park was created, the hills were bare and resembled the landscape of the television programme at the time. Many locals referred to it as 'Teletubby land' to describe the area they were talking about. The name has stuck with a few locals.

Walk 2: A long walk around Gibside

Note – *you need to be a National Trust member or pay at the entrance building to do this walk.*

Distance 4 miles

Time 2 hours

Difficulty Moderate

Parking In the National Trust car park for Gibside off the B6314 from Rowlands Gill to Burnopfield.

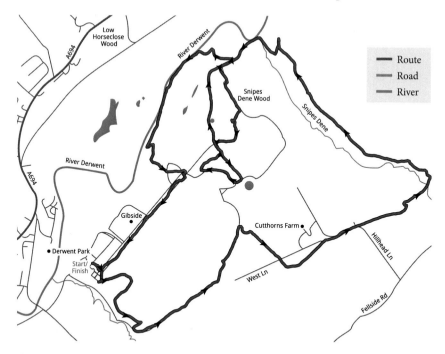

Start

Head for the square where the cafe and toilets are located.

Then head for the steps on to the Long Walk, go diagonally right in front

of the chapel to the start of the pathway to the Strawberry Castle adventure playground.

Follow this path and pass through the adventure playground bearing left to a zig zag path downhill. At the bottom turn left.

Go up the hill and take the left hand fork up the long straight hill. At the top of the hill turn left along the flattish path.

Cut Thorn Farm

Follow the path until you see, on your right, a path signposted 'The Skyline Walk start'. Turn right up through the woodland, across a footbridge and onto a wooden walk way. At the end of this turn right up through a gate then along the edge of a field with fence and drainage trench on your left. Cut Thorn Farm is on your left.

Carry on through a gate, across the track following the pink tulip signs to a stile and on to a further stile. Head on up through the field diagonally left to a fence.

Hillhead

When you reach the fence, walk alongside it on your right to the corner of the field where there is a gate and stile. Stop along here for a while to admire the views across and up the valley – truly stunning. Go over the stile. Turn right along the track past houses on your left – Hillhead house and Hillhead cottages. Just past the garden hedge there is a stile, cross it. Walk along the top of the field with fence on your right. You come to two stiles, take the left hand one. Follow the zig zag path downhill through the woodland with a dene on your left.

At the end there is a gate, go through it and onto the main track with the dene on your left where trees have been felled. Turn right and follow the track downhill for a few hundred metres until you see a path on your left.

Statue of British Liberty

Take the zigzag path downhill with steep ravine on your left until you get to the river. Cross the stone wagonway bridge and follow the path for 50 metres uphill to a clearing. Go straight ahead. Follow the track until you see a path on your left. Take this path uphill through the woods to take you to the statue of British Liberty. You can see it near the top of the hill through the trees on your right.

Take time to enjoy the views and read the information board. Continue on the path away from the statue heading downhill through rhododendron.

Stable block

Carry on downhill until you come to a T junction. Turn left uphill to the top where you'll find the Octagon pond and Banqueting house above it on the hill. Take a look at the pond. Retrace your steps a little and go along the path below the pond going right downhill with the stable block on your left. COFFEE STOP?!

Go downhill on the track and take the first right along a black path and at the end of this walk there is a T junction. Turn left down the hill.

On the right you pass the Lily pond and continue downhill to take the first left path down the zig zag path to the river.

Lady Haugh

Walk along the riverside path. Lady Haugh is on your left.

As you bear away from the river, take the first left doing nearly a U turn up the black path winding uphill to the right of the derelict Gibside Hall.

Gibside Hall and the Long Walk

At the top take the path in front of the hall skirting the natural amphitheatre in front of the hall until you get to the end of the Long walk. Walk along the Long walk to the chapel. End at the steps to the path to a welcome drink at the Potting Shed cafe!

Information

Refreshments

Potting Shed cafe or *Stables cafe* depending on need!!

Gibside is a National Trust country estate, set amongst the peaks and slopes of the Derwent Valley, between Rowlands Gill and Burnopfield. Gibside was previously owned by the Bowes-Lyon family. The main house on the estate is now a shell, but the property is most famous for its chapel. The stables, walled garden and Banqueting House are also intact. The Orangery has recently been refurbished. Details of the history of the estate can be obtained from the shop on the estate.

Walk 3: Turner's Walk through Friarside

Distance   3.7 miles

Time   1 hour and 30 minutes

Difficulty   Moderate in difficulty due to climb from the Derwent Walk to Burnopfield

Parking   Take the road from Rowlands Gill to Burnopfield on the B6134 and in about 300 metres turn right up Stirling Lane and take first left into the car park.

Start

Walk up the path signposted Derwent Walk and onto the viaduct, cross it and continue on up the Derwent Walk for about 300/400 metres and look to your right through the trees to view the remains of Friarside Chapel (this may be difficult to see in summer).

Friarside

At three quarters of a mile you pass under a bridge. Further on you pass a gate on your left marked private. About 150 metres further on at a mile from the viaduct you come to a stile on your left. Cross the stile and walk uphill on a grassy path with newly planted trees on your left and a recently felled woodland on your right.

You come to a stile next to a gate, cross it and follow the path uphill with a hedgerow on your right and at the top of the path you come to a junction between four fields under some overhead electricity cables. Take a left turn with the hedgerow on your right, skirting the top of the field.

Further on you come to an opening at the corner of the field. Take the right hand opening and follow the path to the side of the field with a hedgerow on your left. This path brings you to a gate with an opening to the left between a gate post and a tree.

St James Church, Burnopfield

Turn right up the tarmacked lane. Follow the lane up to the main road and turn left along the path to the side of the road. You pass between St James cemetery on the left – there are some Commonwealth War Graves in this cemetery. St James Church is on the right. Further on to your right is Rai's mini market and the Co-op supermarket for a welcome refreshment.

JMW Turner's painting

About 300 metres further on turn left into Valley View and where the road goes left, carry straight on to take a path to the side of a fence. In about 10 metres bear right to a grassy area. Cross diagonally to the far corner to the view over the valley and take the path down to the top of a field. Follow the path downhill and turn right at the large gap in the hedgerow. Follow the path along the top of the field with hedgerow on your right. You can see Gibside monument in the distance. Somewhere along this path is where JMW Turner painted his famous interpretation of Gibside from the south. Compare the view to the artwork which is in the Bowes Museum, Barnard Castle.

Home

At the end of this field there is a junction where there is a post with two public footpath and public bridleway signs, take the pubic bridleway to a hedgerow enclosed path. Follow this downhill bearing left down the path, ignoring a public footpath sign to your right, and continue until you come to the main road down to Rowlands Gill. Turn left along the path to the side of the road and continue down the path until you come to the bridge at the bottom of the hill just past the entrance to Gibside. Cross the bridge and turn left up the side of the first road ending up in the car park.

Information

Refreshments

The Happiest Sandwich shop, Godley Holme, The Grove, Rowlands Gill, NE39 1PN Tel. 01207 542361

The Kitchen, Station Road, Rowlands Gill NE39 1PZ Tel. 01207 542818

Saltimbocca, Dipwood road, Rowlands Gill, NE39 1BY Tel. 01207 542287

Rai's mini market, 19 The Leazes, Burnopfield NE16 6HR Tel. 01207 272575
Co-op, 20 The Leazes, Burnopfield NE16 6HR Tel. 01207 272827

Friarside Chapel

Friarside Chapel was founded by a hermit called John in about AD 1150. It gave hospitality to pilgrims en route from Jarrow Monastery to Blanchland Abbey. It is now derelict and on private land. There is supposed to be hidden treasure buried in the foundations of the roofless ruin.

Turner's paintings and sketches

JMW Turner painted a number of oils and watercolours and sketched scenes around the Derwent valley near Gibside. Most are in the Tate Gallery and the Bowes Museum.

There are a pair of views of Gibside that were commissioned by the father of the Bowes Museum's founder John Bowes around 1817. Bowes ordered two views of Gibside (one from the north and one from the south) but the stately home appears in neither.

The painting from the south shows a girl carrying a pitcher on her head and in the distance is the chapel, the banqueting house and the column of liberty.

Walk 4: Chopwell Woods and Sculptures

Distance	4.7 miles
Time	2 hours
Difficulty	Moderate
Parking	Park in the lay-by on A694 Lintzford Road just past the Lintzford houses on the left before the bridge over the River Derwent.

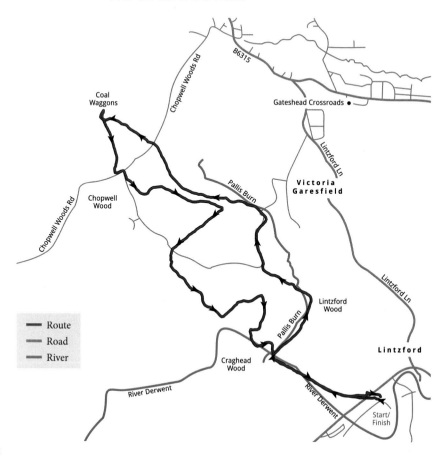

Start

Walk back to the houses and cross the road to the entrance to a lane which is marked as part of the Red Kite trail.

Go through two gates to the lane with hedges on both sides. Follow the lane till you come to the trees. On the left is a large brick tank which is part of some former terraced houses. Carry on to a gate and go through it.

Settling Tanks

Turn second right and follow the path with the stream on the left. You will see several brick walls which were part of the system of settling tanks – see the information boards on your left.

In about 250 metres bear left to cross the stream and immediately up the hill. In 50 metres turn right up the middle track which is a little wider than the other two tracks.

In about 150 metres keep right towards a wide track. On your right is an **owl sculpture**.

Keep right and head up the hill following the wide track till you get to a cross junction with the **Pitman's seat** on your right.

Head straight on ignoring the left and right tracks following the **Pitman's ride**. This track takes you up to a large car park with electricity pylons running above it.

Carry on straight across the car park and the tarmacked road and keep on up the hill till you come to a clearing with several tracks (five exits). You will be turning first left downhill.

Coal waggons

As a detour you could carry on up the hill and take the first right – to view restored Coal waggons.

Go back to where you were and take the left turning mentioned above. When you come to a gate turn left along the tarmacked road and then in about 20 metres right down another tarmacked road.

More wood sculptures

In about 15 metres turn left to a track. Bear right through the trees to a rise and on your left through the trees is an **Orchid sculpture**.

Carry on along this ridge path passing a **Bat sculpture** along the way. At the end of this path is a T junction and a sandy path with a **hand sculpture** to your right. Turn right along this path (**Copper beech avenue**) till you come to another T junction. Head straight across to a narrow path into the trees. Bear left passing the **Guardians sculpture** on your left.

At the end of the path turn left along a wide track and in about 50 metres carry straight on over another wide path onto a narrow path through the trees. When you get to another track turn right and at the bottom of the hill turn right up the hill, then in about 30 metres turn left down the hill till you come to the gate to the approach path and back to the car.

Information

Refreshments

The nearest facilities are at the *entrance to the woodland park* of the B6315 High Spen/Hookergate road. There is a *Cafe in the old Co-op buildings* opposite the entrance. There is also the **Lintzford Garden Centre** on the A694 about 300 metres ahead of the lay-by in which you are parked.

Chopwell Wood is a 360-hectare mixed woodland set on the edge of Gateshead. It has miles of paths for walking, cycling and riding into the heart of this wonderful woodland.

Chopwell Woodland Park was once part of an extensive forest area which covered the countryside from just south of the River Tyne to Allenheads. This so called Wildwood formed about 6,000 years ago and consisted of mixed deciduous trees, mainly oak and hazel.

By the 12th century the wood was part of the Manor of Ceoppa's weille (named by the Saxons) which belonged to the Church. After the dissolution of the monasteries the Crown granted or leased the Manor. Timber from Chopwell was used throughout the 16th and 17th centuries to repair castles and bridges in Northumberland and Durham.

In 1635 over 1,000 trees were marked for construction of a new war ship for King Charles I – 'Sovereign of the Seas', later renamed as 'The Royal Sovereign'. This was the first three-decked sailing war ship.

At the beginning of the l9th century much of the wood was replanted with Oak, but in 1825 an invasion of mice caused a lot of damage by gnawing down many young oaks! Then on January 7th 1839, 20,000 trees were uprooted on 'Windy Monday'. During the second half of the 19th century much of the wood was planted with Larch and some Scots Pine. The wood was drift under-mined in the 19th and early 20th centuries for coal deposits, and a mineral rail-line ran through the wood.

In 1907, Armstrong College, which later became Newcastle University, took on the management of the wood as a demonstration area and training ground for foresters.

In 1919 the Forestry Commission took over management of the wood, with the College still dealing as agents for the current stock. The Transfer of the Woods Act in 1923 gave the Commission full control and they began a full scale replanting programme. Much of the replanting was coniferous, but with some small groups of deciduous trees.

During the Second World War, in October 1941, a German Bomber dropped three high explosive bombs on the Wood, creating three deep craters. These filled with water and have become an excellent wildlife habitat over the years, mainly due to the depth of the original craters!

With the designation of Woodland Park status in 1993, a much greater emphasis has been placed upon conservation and recreation. The commercial forestry is carried out with a more sympathetic manner to these aims. In 2005 the Wood was designated under the PAWS (Plantation on an Ancient Woodland Site) scheme, which prohibits further planting of any trees not native to the area. The Forest Design Plan for Chopwell Wood instructs natural regeneration of species after any felling, or planting of native species only. Keep an eye for deer which are regularly seen in these woods. **(Friends of Chopwell Wood)**

Walk 5: Ebchester (Vindomora) and the Derwentcote Steel furnace

Distance   6.3 miles

Time   2 hours and 15 minutes

Difficulty   Moderate to easy

Parking   Derwent Walk car park at Ebchester station just off Ebchester bank on the B6309.

Grid reference NZ 107 548

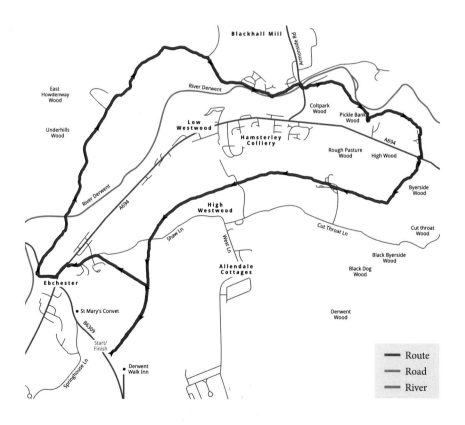

Start

Turn left down the Derwent Walk. Continue for about 300 metres coming to a steep downhill to a cycle control fence/chicane. Go through this chicane and turn left down a public footpath and follow this path down to a lane – this is Shaw Lane.

As you walk down the path, to your right, in the distance, is Milkburnwood which you will walk through later, and to your left, in the distance on the other side of the valley, are the wind turbines at Kiln Pit Hill.

Ebchester

Turn left down Shaw Lane. At the bottom of Shaw Lane are a community centre, school and church on your left.

At the main road, cross over and go past the local shop and immediately on your left you come to a wide gap between the shop and a house. Here you can learn about the history of Ebchester at an information board while standing in the middle of what was the Roman fort of Vindomora.

Go down the hill between the fence and childrens play area and at the end of the stone wall, turn immediately left along a public footpath. Follow the path down the hill until you come to a lane.

River Derwent

Turn right along the lane. Continue past a couple of houses on your right. Further along the path bears right and then left, and at the end of the lane you come to a footbridge across the River Derwent. Cross the bridge.

From here to Blackhall Mill generally keep on the same track ignoring any side tracks or paths.

Cross the field on the obvious path. On the other side of the field you come to a stile by a gate, go through it. Bear left uphill. On the track ahead is a farm.

Head along the track to the farm with hawthorn bushes on your left and gorse on the right and go straight on through the gate at the end of the farm's garden wall.

Follow the track to another gate, cross a stream up to a grassy path to a small hillock, through another field with hawthorn bushes on the left. To your right, over the valley, is **Hamsterley village**.

Carry on to a kissing gate. Go through it to a narrow path with overgrown hawthorn hedges on either side. Continue ahead past a grassy area continuing on a narrow path and bear left through a gate to a lane in about 30 metres.

Blackhall Mill

Turn right along the lane following the line of a stream. At the bottom of the lane you have to turn left into a road. This is Blackhall Mill. You can walk on the grass on the right of the road or on the path to the left of the road. Ignore the footbridge on your right.

Carry on until you come to a main road, turn right across the road bridge.

Cross the road immediately after the bridge and follow the public footpath sign to walk along the side of a fence on your right (do not go along the wide track to your left). This path may be very overgrown in summer so don't be put off. Follow this narrow path for a few hundred metres. Walk along the river bank to the end of the fence line into a woodland and the path bears to the right away from the river and in 20 metres turn left up a wide stony path with a stream on your right.

Derwentcote Steel Furnace

At the top of this lane is a house. Take a U turn on the path to a grassy area. Cross this area to a narrow gap between two fences. At the end of the path is a stile. Go through the stile and follow the path across the field past a large oak on your left and head for the wood in the distance where you will see a fence with a stile in the middle – cross it to another stile within five metres. This brings you to a stream. Cross the stream and bear right up the track. This brings you to the Derwentcote steel furnace. Pause to have a look – it's free, but the building itself is only open on certain occasions.

Carry on up the track with a house on your right on rough tarmac track to the main road. Turn right and within a few metres, cross the road to a stile and public footpath.

Derwent Walk

Follow the path with trees and stream to your right until you come to an opening in the tree line to a stile. Cross the stile and through the wood, crossing a stream, heading uphill. This can be a muddy path. At the top of the hill you come to the Derwent Walk, turn right and follow it for about two miles arriving back at the car park.

Information

Refreshments

You can treat yourself to drink and food at either the *Derwent Walk Inn* or the *Riverview Bakery. The Derwent Walk Inn* is just above the car park on the main road. At the bottom of Ebchester bank is the *Chelmsford pub* or *'The Knack',* as it is locally known.

Derwent Walk Inn, Ebchester Hill, Consett, Co. Durham DH8 0SX Tel. 01207 560347. Food is served daily between 12pm-9pm Monday to Friday and 11.30am-9pm Saturday, Sunday and Bank Holidays.

Riverview Bakery, 14 River view, Blackhall Mill Tel. 01207 563668

Vindomora (or Ebchester Roman Fort) was probably an earth and timber fort built in about AD 80 to protect Dere street. The stone fort was built in AD163 but was abandoned in AD410. Little remains of the fort as the village was built directly on top of it. Roman remains are spread amongst the gardens, cottages, roads and St Ebba's Church. Parts of the walls are still visible near the post office.

(Wikipedia)

Derwentcote Steel furnace was built in the 1730s and was used for cementation, a process which converted wrought iron into steel.

It is one of the few complete examples of this type of furnace, and is the last surviving piece of evidence of cementation steelmaking in the north-east.

The conical chimney houses two sandstone chests into which iron bars were packed with alternate layers of charcoal powder.

When the fire was lit and the chests sealed, flames and heat travelled up through flues and chimneys around them, and temperatures reached 1,100°C. This heat enabled the carbon from the charcoal to diffuse into the iron.

Each cementation cycle, or 'heat', took three weeks, producing about 10 tons of steel. The firing took 6 - 10 days and the furnace was then allowed to cool for a week, before the bars could be extracted.

These bars of 'blister steel' were taken to the nearby water-powered forge, to be made into items such as cutting tools and springs. The steel had remarkable flexibility and strength, and was said to be of excellent quality.

The Derwent valley was the centre of the British steel industry in the early 18th century, as it had all the natural resources needed for the cementation process. It had plentiful supplies of charcoal, coal, clay and sandstone, and easy access to the North Sea for the import of Swedish iron.

Derwentcote furnace went out of use by 1891 and subsequently fell into disrepair. It was restored by English Heritage in 1990.
(http://www.english-heritage.org.uk)

Walk 6: Ebchester, Newlands, Shotley Bridge, Derwent Walk

Distance   6 miles

Time   2.25 to 2.5 hours

Difficulty   Moderate to easy

Parking   Derwent walk car park at Ebchester station just off Ebchester bank on the B6309.

Grid reference NZ 107 548

Start

Walk down the Derwent Walk track heading east towards Rowlands Gill. Carry on down a dip to a cycle calming measure and turn left down a track.

As you turn into the path you will see three wind turbines near Whittonstall and the Kiln Pit hill wind turbines across the valley in the distance.

Ebchester

At the bottom of the track turn left along Shaw Lane passing St Ebba's church on your left. At the junction to the main road (Vindomora Road) cross the road and go past the shop, turning left and carry on between the fence and the children's playground then turn left immediately after the fence line/stone wall ends. Follow the track downhill to a lane, turn left along the lane with a stone garden and house wall to your right.

When you come to the main road, cross it, turn right and in about 30 metres you come to an old road on your left which crosses an old stone bridge. Cross this bridge. Look up river to see a weir. Follow the road up the hill to the main road.

Newlands

When you come to the main road, cross it and turn left along the wide grassy area (in summer the grass can be long) and carry on up the road to the junction

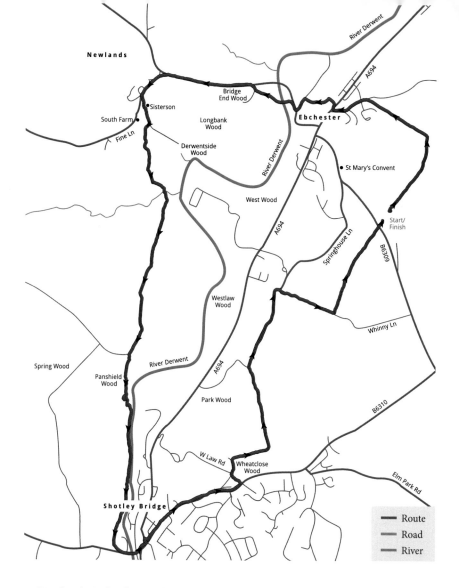

Route — Road — River

to Newlands. Take the road left, signposted Carterway Heads 4 miles and Shotley Field 2¾ miles. Follow the road for about 150m and bear left in front of some houses (public right of way sign to Panshields 1¼ miles Shotley Bridge 2¼ miles).

Secret waterfalls

At the end of the houses follow the track and bear right to enter the woodland, keeping the fence on your left and river gorge on your right. At the bottom of

the hill, cross the stone bridge (which is above a waterfall). Follow the track left up to a gate and stile. Bear right up the hill and at the top of the field you will see a stile and a gate in the diagonal corner of a field, head for the stile and cross it. Turn left following the ravine on your right, follow the zig zag path downhill to a wooden bridge (which is above another waterfall). Follow the path uphill to a gate to a field.

Panshields

Cross the field heading for the farm buildings in the distance. Pass through a gap in the hedge after crossing the first field and cross a stile after the second field. Bearing left and in about 150m before the farm buildings (Panshields) there is a gate in the corner of the field leading on to a farm track. Go through the gate and follow the track to the farm buildings. At the end of the farm buildings bear left downhill into a woodland and follow the path through it. Carry on downhill with a pond on your right and head for the path along the riverside.

Shotley Bridge

On the other side of the river you will see Shotley Bridge Cricket Club where Paul Collingwood (a former England captain) was a junior. Follow the path for about half a mile until you come to a stone stile and a road. Turn left along the road to the stone bridge across the river leading to Shotley Bridge. Go up the hill and cross the road carrying on uphill to Snows Green Road.

You could pause in the centre of Shotley Bridge at the various pubs and restaurants. Carry on up the hill passing the former Town Hall on your left. Further on, Our Lady of the Rosary catholic church is on your right carrying on to Shotley Bridge Junior School on your left.

Derwent Walk and home

About 100 metres past the road to Benfieldside (a road to your right) turn first left at a tiny house carrying on uphill along West Law Road. This road takes you past an unusual house with a clock on the outbuilding – Snows Green house. Follow this road for about a mile. When you come to a sign – Springhouse Lane – turn right off the road and follow a track uphill for a few hundred metres until you come to signs for the Derwent Walk. Turn left down the Derwent Walk for about a half a mile to the car park where you started.

Information

Refreshments

Crown and Cross Swords, Front Street, Shotley Bridge, Consett DH8 0HU
Tel. 01207 502 006
Isabella's Coffee shop, 8 Front Street, Shotley Bridge DH8 0HH
Tel. 01207 655100
Sale Pepe, 10-12 Front Street, Shotley Bridge, Consett DH8 0HH
Tel. 01207 509 969
Kings Head, Front Street, Shotley Bridge, Consett, County Durham, DH8 0HX
Tel: 01207 583899

Roman Ebchester

Modern day Ebchester overlies the Roman fort Vindomora which was first built in AD 80. The name Vindomora, derived from the Celtic language, means 'Black Moor Edge'.

The fort and permanent settlement were built when the Roman road, Dere Street, was extended north from York to Corbridge. The fort accommodated up to 500 soldiers and provided an overnight staging-post on the route north for over 300 years.

The rampart of the first fort at Ebchester can be seen in the Vindomora playground on the north side of the Newcastle to Shotley Bridge road and also the site and curve of the rampart and angle turret on the west corner of the

fort site. The commandant's house is under Mains Farm behind which are the remains of the bath house, containing part of the hypocaust heating system. When the bath house was excavated in 1962 it was found to date to the fourth century and some of the floor was still in-situ. Two further rooms were discovered inside farm buildings and suggest that the house was possibly of the courtyard type with a range of rooms around its perimeter. The headquarters building is under Shaw Lane, immediately outside the churchyard gateway. Two large cubic bases from the western portico of this building are now under the gateposts into the churchyard. (**www.ebchester.org**)

Shotley Bridge

The origins of swordmaking here dated from 1691. A group of Lutheran swordmakers from Solingen in Germany settled in Shotley Bridge, allegedly in order to escape religious persecution, though in practice their departure was prompted by their breaking of guild oaths. Shotley Bridge was probably chosen because of the rich iron deposits in the area and because of the fast flowing waters of the River Derwent, providing hydraulic power for hammers and grinders. Another factor may have been the remoteness of the area, as the swordmakers were keen to preserve their trade secrets, those that they had illegally taken with them from Germany. The swordmakers were able to employ the services of the famous local engraver Thomas Bewick. Swords are no longer made in the Shotley Bridge district. Before the last remaining cottages occupied by the swordmakers were torn down, there was an inscription over the door of one reading "Das Herren segen machet reich ohn alle Sorg wenn Du zugleich in deinem Stand treu und fleissig bist und tuest alle vas die befolen ist". This is from the Lutheran belief code and means that God's benefits will be given without reserve to those who stand firm in their belief no matter what happens. (**Wikipedia**)

Walk 7: Shotley Bridge to Hownsgill viaduct via Allensford

Distance   7 miles

Time   2.5 hours

Difficulty   Moderate

Parking   Heading towards Blackhill from Shotley Bridge on the A691 before you rise up the hill turn right onto Shotley Grove Road and follow the road as far as you can go. There is a free car park next to a new footbridge.

Start

Cross the bridge next to the car park and turn left along the path with the river on your left. Follow this path, keeping close to the river, ignoring paths to the right, to Allensford (about 1.5 miles). Along the way you pass a weir.

Allensford

As you approach Allensford with the caravan park on the other side of the river you will follow the path uphill through a wood and very near to the end of this path there is a small bridge over a stream before coming to a main road (this is the A68). Turn left at the main road downhill to a bridge and take the first left with the house on your right. The large expanse of grass in front of you is Allensford Park. Head for the buildings in the distance.

Allensford Woods

When you get to the caravan site entrance, to the right is the entrance to the Allensford Woods. Follow this path and very quickly go uphill to your right. This path zig zags uphill until you come to a road. Cross the road and follow the path through the wood, with the burn on your left, for about 3/4 mile ending up near a school and a road.

Turn right and cross the road and walk up the hill on the path. When you get to St John's church hall which is on your right, turn left and in about 300 metres, cross the main road. On crossing the road there is a public footpath sign to your right. Follow this path until you get to some steps. Go up the steps and follow the path with some houses on your right and bear left across a rough field to the corner of the field and head into a woodland and follow the steps uphill which bears left up the escarpment to a stile at the top.

Hownsgill Viaduct

Cross the stile and turn left, following the edge of the field along the top of the escarpment for a few hundred metres until you come to another stile into a small wood. Go through this wood to the Hownsgill viaduct which you can see on your left. Walk across the viaduct and after about 200m take the path to the left under a small bridge and walk on to the Hownsgill junction where you can find a slag wagon from the former Consett Iron works.

Derwent Walk

This junction is the start of the Derwent Walk and the Lanchester cycleway and part of the C2C cycle way. Here you could have a break at the Hownsgill Tea Rooms, open every day 9-4 except Tuesdays.

Turn immediately left onto the Derwent Walk. Carry on down the track and to a road. Turn right and in about 300m take the path to the right taking you to a main road. Cross it and follow the path to another road, cross it and enter the path crossing a stile. Follow it for about 300-400 m and bear slightly left between two gate posts. Continue along this path until you follow the contour of the hill for about half a mile or so until you come to some more gate posts. Continue until you come to bear left downhill and cross a field diagonally to an opening in the fence next to a covered reservoir.

Home

Turn left down the road and in about 200m turn right down a path and continue along this path for about 3/4 of a mile until you come to a tarmacked lane. Turn left down the hill and when you get to the bottom turn immediately left (signposted free car park 200m) along the lane past the garage and into the car park.

Information

Refreshments – *Hownsgill Tea rooms*, Hownsgill Farm, Consett DH8 9AA Tel. 01207 503597

Crown and Cross Swords, Front Street, Shotley Bridge, Consett DH8 0HU Tel. 01207 502 006

Sale Pepe, 10-12 Front Street, Shotley Bridge, Consett DH8 0HH Tel. 01207 509 969

Kings Head, Front Street, Shotley Bridge, Consett, County Durham, DH8 0HX
Tel: 01207 583899
Isabella's 8 Front Street, Shotley Bridge, Consett 077496 540062

Hownsgill Viaduct

The Stockton & Darlington Railway proposed to build a bridge at Hownes Gill and they commissioned Thomas Bouch to design and supervise its construction. Bouch's design was submitted to Robert Stephenson, who recommended the use of inverted arches under the five central piers to reduce ground loading.

John Anderson started works in 1857 with three million white firebricks being used in the structure, with sandstone Ashlar dressings, and iron railings along the platform. The completed single-track bridge opened in 1858, 700 feet (210m) long and at maximum 150 feet (46m) high, spanned by twelve 50 feet (15m) wide arches on slender triple-tiered piers, with arched recesses in three layers on each side.

The railway line was fully closed in the early 1980s, with the tracks lifted by 1985.

The bridge is now part of the Sustrans national foot and cycle path network as part of the Sea to Sea Cycle Route, which crosses from Whitehaven/ Workington on the west coast to Sunderland/Tynemouth on the east coast. In 2013 anti-suicide fences were fitted to the bridge; there was one suicide from the bridge every two weeks in the first half of 2011 and five between January and August 2012. (**Wikipedia**)

Walk 8: Derwent Gorge and Muggleswick Woods

Distance	5 Miles
Time	2-2.5 hours
Difficulty	Moderate to easy
Parking	Allensford car park immediately next to the A68. To reach this, going north on the A68 turn right before the bridge across the River Derwent; going south turn left after the bridge.

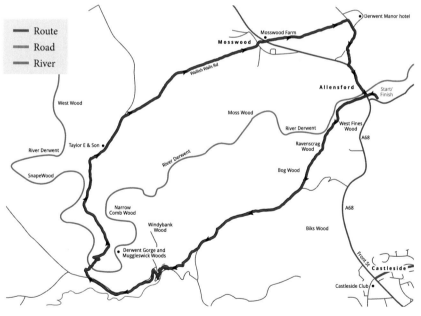

Start

Walk behind the bungalows next to the A68 and cross it with the bridge on your right. There is a public footpath between a white bungalow and number 337's drive. Follow the path with a tall wooden fence on your right and a metal

fence on your left to a gate. Follow the path to a stream coming from your left and cross the bridge over the stream (note the waterfall to your left) and bear left up the hill on a track through the trees. At the top of the wood there is a stile, go over it and follow the line of hawthorn bushes on your left.

Derwent Grange farm

Head for a gate opening (stone and wood gate posts) with wooded hillside on your right and continue until you come to another gate. Go through it and turn right up the tarmaced road passing Derwent Grange farm on your right. Pass through two gates and pass Foxholes (a house) on your left and after about 300 metres there is a stile on your right with public footpath sign. Go over it and follow path (ignoring the temptation to go down steeply towards the river) downhill through the wood to another stile and into a field. Bear right across the field another stile in the corner of the field to more woodland, follow path downhill to a gate and onto the road again.

Follow the road across two bridges and head up the hair pin bends, but you could cut the road and hair pin bends out by going through a number of gates straight up the hill through the trees.

When you reach the top of the hill continue for about 300-400 metres ignoring the first public footpath sign until you see a gate signposting another public footpath on your right. Follow this sign.

Muggleswick Woods and the Derwent Gorge

Follow the path downhill to another small sign 'Natural England' on the right for a path into the Derwent Gorge and Muggleswick Woods national nature reserve. Continue down the zig zag path to a footbridge, cross it and pass the farmhouse with it on your left and turn right on the track and follow the track up to Crooked Oak (three houses) (in about one mile).

Wallish Walls

Continue past these houses until you come to a fork in the road and take the right fork along Wallish Walls Road past three large barns of Wallish Walls farm.

About half a mile past the barns you come to a T junction in the road. On your left is the Mosswood water treatment works. Turn left and immediately across the road on your right there is a gate. Go through it across the small field to another gate (this field may be overgrown and if so head for the A68 main road on the side road). Cross the A68 to the gate (or, if you want to shorten the walk, turn right along the roadside path to Allensford – about half a mile). Go through the gate (opening) and follow the public footpath alongside the field and head in a straight line for the buildings in the distance. Head for the right hand gap in the wall and follow the path with the wall on your left. The buildings are the Derwent Manor Hotel. When you get to the hotel pass the swimming pool with it on your left.

Home

Turn right on the road, follow the road to the A68 and turn left on the footpath down the hill to the bridge at Allensford and back into the car park.

Information

Refreshments

Allensford shop, Allensford Caravan Park, Pemberton Road, Castleside, Consett DH8 9BA Tel. 01207 593 624

Best Western Derwent Manor Hotel, Allensford, Northumberland, DH8 9BB Tel:01207 59200

Derwent Gorge and Muggleswick Woods national nature reserve

This is a Site of Special Scientific Interest (SSSI). It consists of two separate areas of woodland, one in the gorge of the River Derwent and the other in the ravine of its tributary, the Horsleyhope Burn.

In the dry acidic soils of the upper slopes, the woodland is dominated by sessile oak, *Quercus petraea*. Some areas have been coppiced in the past but where the slopes are steepest, and least accessible, there appears to have been no human interference. **(Wikipedia)**

Derwent Gorge & Muggleswick Woods NNR hosts a diversity of wildlife with particularly rich bird and plant communities. There is a large area of ancient sessile oakwood with a bird community typical of upland woods, including Redstart, Pied Flycatcher and Wood Warbler.

Much of the site is designated as an SSSI, partly for its epiphytic flora, including a diverse range of lichens, and there are also herb-rich grasslands around the woodland edges. **(http://www.cieem.net)**

Walk 9: Derwent dam, Edmundbyers and Muggleswick

Distance   7.7 miles

Time   3 hours

Difficuty   Moderate

Parking   Northumbrian Water car park off the B6278. This is the car park at the bottom of the dam. It is on the right before you cross the bridge going towards Edmundbyers.

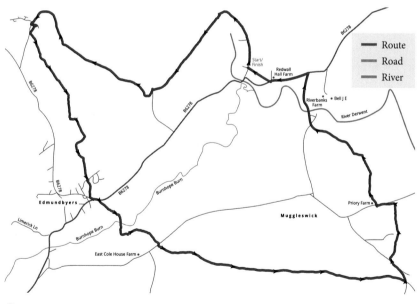

Start

Walk uphill on the road towards some trees; the road continues onto the Derwent Reservoir dam. Walk across the top of the dam. On the other side take the second of two gates on your right signposted Pow Hill Country Park and walk down to a bridge, cross it and continue on the path next to the reservoir

edge through several gates until you have to turn left away from the reservoir uphill towards the car park next to the Pow Hill picnic site. Walk up the road to the brow of the first hill and turn left through a gate to a Cafe. Walk down the drive to the stile in the fence, cross it to another stile and stone stile immediately after.Walk across several boggy fields taking the line of the electricity poles.

Edmundbyers

When you get to a line of hawthorn bushes, bear right to the corner of a field to a gate. Go through it and head for the buildings in the distance, aiming for the green telephone box. Cross the stile near the caravan site and turn right up the lane and then to the main road.

You could pause for refreshments at the Village shop, the Punch Bowl pub or The Baa micro pub. Turn left at the main road past the Low House Haven building and immediately after it turn right to a public footpath.

Pass through the gate with the caravan site on your right.

Continue downhill for about 100 metres following the fence line and head right downhill to a wooden footbridge across a stream.

Muggleswick Park

Cross the bridge and head uphill towards a house and in 200 metres before a stile turn left alongside a stone wall and head for the obvious path. As you climb the hill look right up to a stile in the fence beyond the tree line. Climb up the hill to the stile and head across the field to a gap in a wall to the right of the left one of two electricity poles and then to a gate before coming to a well tarmacked road. Cross it and to your right is a public footpath sign. Follow this track up to and across Muggleswick Park (the moor).

At the top of this moor you can see almost the entire Derwent valley from the reservoir to Newcastle. This is one of the most spectacular views in the valley.

Muggleswick

At the end of this track is a road – turn left along it for about 300 metres ignoring the first public footpath sign on your right and take the second public footpath sign going through a gate and following the fence line on your right. Head for the stile ahead, cross it and the track to another stile following the fence line on your right to a gate. Continuing on you come to the gate to a churchyard. Go through the churchyard to another gate and a grassy path to another gate. Turn right after the gate and in about 30 metres turn left through another gate. (Here you could detour slightly to view the ruins of Muggleswick Manor.)

Continue with a house and stone wall on your left and head uphill to a gate in the wall. Turn right alongside the stone wall to a stile. Keeping the wall on your right carry on to another stile, bear left to cross another field, crossing another two stiles keeping to the contour of the land. Head diagonally left across the field to and over the wall stile. Continue in the same direction to another stile above the farm. Continue across the top of the field to a gate and ahead is a road.

Eddy's bridge and home

Turn right down hill to Eddy's bridge crossing the River Derwent and follow the road to a road junction. Turn left and walk along the grass verge until about 30 metres past the entrance to Redwell Hall Farm. Take public footpath signed Birkenside to the right and go up to a gate. Bear right and head for another gate turn left to the gate in the left corner of the field. Through the gate is the car park where you started.

Information

Refreshments – *The Punch Bowl Inn, Edmundbyers, Consett, DH8 9NL Tel. 01207 255545*
The Old Village Shop, Edmundbyers, Consett DH8 9NL Tel. 01207 255 394
Derwent Reservoir shop, Edmundbyers, Consett DH8 9TT Tel. 01207 255 250
The Baa, Edmundbyers, DH8 9NL. Tel. 01207 255651

Edmundbyers

Dates back to the 11th century, as the name 'Edmundbyers' comes from the Old English for 'Eadmunds byre or barn'. The village itself was first recorded in the early 12th century in the Bolden Book. By this time the church of St Edmund's had been built.

There are the ruins of a priory, once a hunting lodge for the Prior of Durham, which is a listed building. These are located near to the church.
(http://www.keystothepast.info) (Wikipedia)

Muggleswick Common or Park

A significant area of the south and west of the village is taken up by Muggleswick Common, an area of upland moorland used for grouse rearing (and associated game (food) shooting) and sheep grazing. This area consists predominately of heather with encroaching bracken. The Common is part of the Muggleswick, Stanhope and Edmundbyers Commons and Blanchland Moor Site of Special Scientific Interest (SSSI). **(Wikipedia)**

Derwent Reservoir

Derwent Reservoir was formed by an earth dam across the River Derwent, a tributary of the River Tyne, and forms the county boundary between Northumberland and County Durham. Water from the reservoir flows through 2.2 miles of twin 41 inch diameter pipeline to the treatment works near Mosswood. The treatment works includes sedimentation tanks, filters and a laboratory. The water then travels 27 miles to Washington to be distributed to customers in Durham, Sunderland and South Tyneside.

The reservoir collects the water running off 27,200 acres (110km²) of catchment. The average rainfall of the catchment is 37.5 inches (953mm). The reservoir provides a reliable daily yield of 30.5 million gallons (112,320 cubic meters per day). Compensation water is discharged to the river below the dam at an average rate of 5.75 million gallons a day, leaving a balance for each undertaking of 12.5 million gallons a day.

The reservoir is one of the largest inland waters in England. It is 3.5 miles (5.6 km) long and covers an area of 1,000 acres (4 km²). The maximum depth of the water is 100 ft (30m) at the dam, and when full the reservoir will hold 11,000 million gallons (50 million m³).

Three farmsteads, two cottages and a charming old house, known as Millshield Mill, were demolished before the reservoir was filled. Two miles of public road were submerged but were replaced by four miles of new road.

Construction of the reservoir, which cost £5.5 million, started in 1960 and water was first taken into supply in September 1966.

The earth dam is 3,000 ft (914m) long and 119ft (36m) high above old river bed level.

The volume of the dam is 2.6 million cubic yards (2 million m³). All the earth for making it was dug from the area, now under water, together with sand and gravel for most of the concrete. There are around 750,000 bricks in the dam wall.

Before a dam could be built, the River Derwent had to be diverted through a tunnel 17ft in diameter and 646 yds long. When the dam was built, the tunnel was plugged with concrete 25ft thick. Upstream of the plug the tunnel is now full of water, while downstream it is dry and contains the pipes through which the water is taken from the reservoir. (**https://www.nwl.co.uk**)

Walk 10:
Carrick to Baybridge via Blanchland

Distance 4.5 miles

Time 1.5 hours plus

Difficulty Easy

Parking Follow the B6306 from Edmundbyers to Blanchland.
Follow the signs to the former Carrick picnic site
about 1 mile before Blanchland. Park on the road side.

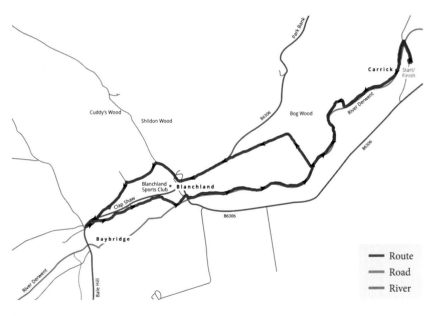

Start

Walk away from the steep hill towards the bridge. Immediately after the bridge
turn left along the public footpath signposted Blanchland 1.5 miles.

The path takes you through woodland and through open grassy areas
alongside the river. Follow the way markers signs. When you get to a three way

sign post, take the Blanchland ¾ mile direction away from the river and follow it up to a road. Carry on left along the road towards Blanchland.

Blanchland

After about 50 metres cross the road onto a path on the right hand side of the road. Follow it to the centre of the village and turn right between the White Monk tea rooms and the houses opposite signposted to the village car park.

Ignore the car park and walk up the road until you come to a left turn in the road to Cote House farm which is signposted ¼ mile.

Follow that road to the top of the hill and as you turn towards the farm there is a public footpath sign on your left. Go through the gate and into a small field, cross it to a stile over a stone wall bear left along a grassy path.

Baybridge

You soon head downhill to another stile over a stone wall next to a gate. When you cross it there is a road, turn right and within about 50 metres there is a permissive path on your left. The houses of Baybridge are to your right. Turn into the path and follow it for about half a mile until you come to a gate to a football pitch. Cross the pitch diagonally to your right towards a children's play area, head to path between the play area and the river, then across a wooden bridge and diagonally left to a gap in the stone wall.

Home

Turn right and cross the road and immediately after the bridge and before the public toilets turn right between the bridge and the toilets. Follow the river path along to Carrick for about 1 ¾ miles.

Information

Refreshments

The White Monk Tearooms, The Old School, Blanchland, Consett, County
Durham DH8 9ST Tel: 01434 675044
Lord Crewe Arms, The Square, Blanchland, Consett DH8 9SP Tel.01434 675 469
Blanchland Village Shop, The Square, Blanchland, Consett DH8 9SR
Tel. 01434 675209

Blanchland

Blanchland was formed out of the medieval Blanchland Abbey property by
Nathaniel Crew, 3rd Baron Crew, the Bishop of Durham, 1674-1722. It is a
conservation village, largely built of stone from the remains of the 12th century
Abbey. The picturesque houses are set against a backdrop of deep woods and
open moors.

   The Lord Crewe Arms Hotel has a vast fireplace where 'General' Tom
Forster hid during the Jacobite rising of 1715. W. H. Auden stayed at the Lord
Crewe Arms with Gabriel Carritt at Easter 1930 and later remarked that no
place held sweeter memories. Blanchland may have been the model for the
village in which was set the opening and closing scenes of Auden and
Isherwood's play The Dog Beneath the Skin (1935). Another celebrated poet
Philip Larkin used to dine at the hotel when staying with Monica Jones in
Haydon Bridge. In July 1969, Benjamin Britten and Peter Pears stayed at the
Inn. **(Wikipedia)**

Walk 11: Near the source – Beldon Burn and Nookton Burn

Distance	10 miles
Time	4 hours
Difficulty	Moderate
Parking	Blanchland car park

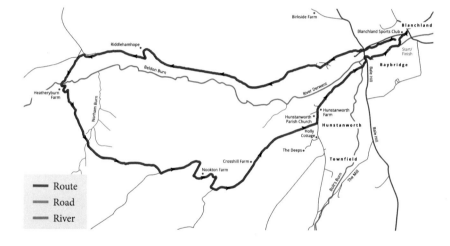

Start

Walk back down the road into the centre of Blanchland and turn first right and in about 100m take the gate into the football field on the left and head for another gate to a path. Follow the path to Baybridge.

Baybridge

On reaching Baybridge bear right across the road to the entrance to Newbiggin Hall. Don't be put off by the Private sign on the right stone pillar, there is a public footpath sign to the left of the entrance. This is a public footpath to Hunstanworth 1.5 miles and Riddlehamhope 3 miles.

Newbiggin

Walk up this well tarmacked road past a church on your right and up
the hill. When you reach the buildings of **Newbiggin** go through the first gate
straight ahead with farm buildings on your left and stone wall to the right. In
about 100 metres the track goes right. Follow the track to another gate with
open field on your right and stone wall on your left. Carry on through another
gate. Soon after there is a footpath sign pointing left. This is where you could
shorten your route and head downhill to the river (**Beldon Burn**) where you
will find a ford and a footbridge joining the longer route at Hunstanworth.

If you wish to do the longer walk ignore this path and head straight on
following the path through another gate. Continue to another gate and into a
wood. Carry on this track for about ¾ of a mile to a gate.

Riddlehamhope

Through the gate the track goes downhill to a stile. Cross it and bear left uphill.
Carry on to a grassy path towards Riddlehamhope. You cross a stile into a wood
and go through a couple of gates to the derelict buildings of **Riddlehamhope.**
Pass these buildings with them on your left, through another gate and bear
right up the hill with the stone wall on your right. You come to two gates, take
the one straight ahead and turn left to an obvious track and follow this along
the line of the stone wall downhill. At the bottom you cross the river (**Beldon
Burn**) onto the track to **Heatheryburn farm**. Go through the gate and turn

immediately left through another gate and right through another and onto the path which winds uphill to another gate bringing you onto **Nookton Fell.**

As you cross the moor through a couple of gates on your left is a **Shooting cabin**. Carry on along the track for about 2 miles. Head downhill to your right following the line of a stone wall.

Hunstanworth

Go through the gate to the farm and head through the farmyard and in about 150 metres take the obvious track downhill to a bridge, and bearing left take the tarmacked road, following this road along to Hunstanworth passing **Wagtail and Cross hill farms**. When you get to the T junction turn left down to the beautiful hamlet of **Hunstanworth**. Carry on the road downhill to Baybridge. Just after the bridge across the river turn immediately right on the public footpath alongside the river. Follow this path to Blanchland. Just before you get to the football field there is a gap in the wall – head for the field and then for the gate diagonally right and pass through the gate onto the road into **Blanchland** and back up to the car park.

Information

Refreshments – *The White Monk Tearooms*, The Old School, Blanchland, Consett, County Durham DH8 9ST Tel: 01434 675044
Lord Crewe Arms, The Square, Blanchland, Consett DH8 9SP Tel.01434 675 469
Blanchland Village shop, The Square, Blanchland, Consett DH8 9SR Tel. 01434 675209

Hunstanworth

The village was designed and built around the original 1781 parish church. The Reverend Daniel Capper commissioned architect Samuel Sanders Teulon to create the village in the 1860s, and Teulon delivered a vicarage and stable block, school and school-house and a mix of terraced, semi-detached and detached houses, all constructed of sandstone. Hunstanworth is one of the Thankful Villages that suffered no fatalities during the Great War of 1914-1918. **(Wikipedia)**